CHOOSING AN ASSISTED LIVING FACILITY

UNDERSTANDING ASSISTED LIVING FOR SENIORS AND THEIR FAMILY

JACKIE LEROY

ISBN:9798325778612

DEDICATION

I dedicate this book to my darling wife Charlie. In life, I loved you dearly. In death, I love you still and, in my heart, you hold a place no one else will ever fill.

CONTENT CONTENTS

CHAPTER 1: INTRODUCTION

In the intricate tapestry of life, there comes a time when the threads of independence and care interweave, guiding us towards new chapters filled with warmth, companionship, and support. As the golden years unfurl, the journey towards retirement and aging gracefully prompts reflection on the spaces we inhabit and the communities we nurture.

Within this mosaic of aging experiences, assisted living facilities emerge as sanctuaries of comfort and vitality, offering a haven where seniors can thrive amidst compassionate care and enriching engagements. This book seeks to illuminate the path towards understanding and embracing the multifaceted world of assisted living facilities; a realm where dignity, autonomy, and quality of life converge to create vibrant living environments for our cherished senior citizens.

Through these pages, we embark on a journey of exploration, delving into the ethos, practices, and nuances that define assisted living facilities. From the fundamental principles underpinning resident-centered care to the diverse array of amenities and services tailored to meet individual needs, we traverse the landscape of assisted living with reverence and insight.

Drawing upon the wisdom of experts, the stories of residents, and the dedication of caregivers, this book serves as a beacon of knowledge and empowerment for those navigating the transition to assisted living, as well as for families seeking clarity and guidance in their quest to provide the best possible support for their loved ones.

As we navigate the pages ahead, may we embrace the spirit of compassion, empathy, and advocacy that defines the essence of assisted living, fostering a community where every individual is celebrated, cherished, and empowered to live life to the fullest.

Welcome to the journey; a journey of discovery, understanding and celebration of the beauty and the resilience of the human spirit in its' golden years.

CHAPTER 2: WHY THIS BOOK

Good morning reader. It is January 25, 2024. This Wisconsin weather is cloudy with some snow still on the ground. I have chosen this day to start writing my newest book called: "Choosing An Assisted Living Facility: Understanding Assisted Living for Seniors and Their Family."

The reason I have decided to write this book is I first experienced my father and mother living in an assisted living facility and my family serving as helpers for them. Neither my parents nor my family had any experience with assisted living facilities. Next came my wife's parents in assisted living with my wife and I as helpers. You may say we had a little experience as helpers, but very limited knowledge of what my in-laws were experiencing daily.

My wife passed on and I was living alone. You might say I had a few tasks daily that would have been easier with another set of helping hands. Eventually my family suggested it was time I consider a different living arrangement. I was willing to do this but was not aware of what the daily routine of an assisted living facility would be like. But I was willing to give it a try.

It now has been almost four years since I entered my first facility. I have learned a lot and believe it is worth sharing what I have experienced with other senior citizens.

I believe the most limiting factor most senior citizens make is entering such care facilities without a clear understanding of what this change in living is all about. That my friends is the reason for this book.

I will do my best to share with you the process that one should consider when changing a new living environment.

CHAPTER 3: ASSISTED LIVING DEFINITION

Let us begin with a clear definition of an assisted living facility (ALF). An ALF is not a nursing home or a memory care facility. Many ALF's house residents in need of assisted living, independent living or memory care, however, they live in different sections of the facility. What then is an ALF? An ALF is a residential housing option designed for seniors who require assistance with activities of daily living (ADL) such as bathing, dressing, medication management, and meal preparation, but who do not require the intensive medical care provided in nursing homes.

ALFs provide a supportive environment where residents can maintain a level of independence while receiving personalized care and support tailored to their individual needs. These facilities typically offer a range of services and amenities, including 24-hour staffing, housekeeping, transportation, social activities, and access to healthcare professionals.

The goal of an ALF is to promote autonomy, dignity, and quality of life for residents while ensuring their safety and well-being in a home-like setting. Now that the reader has an initial briefing of just what an ALF is, let us begin the process of evaluating what you may want for a future living situation.

CHAPTER 4: EVALUATING AN ASSISTED LIVING FACILITY

Think of the following as a guide. **Do not let this list overwhelm you as we will get into the actual evaluation as we continue, and we will get into the how to as we move forward.**

When choosing an ALF for yourself or a loved one, several factors should be carefully considered to ensure the best possible fit and quality of care. Here are some important factors to consider:

- **<u>Location:</u>** Consider the proximity of the facility to family members, friends, medical facilities, and amenities such as shopping centers and parks. A convenient location can facilitate visits and access to essential services.

- **<u>Licensing and Accreditation:</u>** Verify that the ALF is properly licensed and accredited by relevant regulatory agencies. This ensures that the facility meets certain standards of care and safety.

- **<u>Services and Amenities:</u>** Evaluate the range of services and amenities offered by the facility, including assistance with activities of daily living (ADLs), medication management, meal provision, housekeeping, transportation, social activities, and access to healthcare professionals.

- **<u>Staffing and Training:</u>** Inquire about the qualifications, training, and ratio of staff to residents. Adequate staffing levels and well-trained caregivers are essential for providing quality care and attention to residents' needs.

- **<u>Care Plans and Personalization:</u>** Discuss how care plans are developed and personalized to meet each residents' unique needs and preferences. Look for facilities that involve residents and their families in care planning and decision-making processes.

- **Safety and Security:** Assess the safety and security measures in place within the facility, including emergency response protocols, security features, and supervision of residents with cognitive impairments or mobility issues.

- **Cleanliness and Maintenance:** Observe the cleanliness and maintenance of the facility during visits. A clean and well-maintained environment is essential for promoting health, comfort, and overall well-being.

- **Social and Recreational Activities:** Consider the availability of social, recreational, and educational activities tailored to residents' interests and abilities. Engaging activities can enhance quality of life and foster a sense of community and belonging.

- **Resident Reviews and Feedback:** Seek out reviews and feedback from current and former residents, as well as their families, to gain insights into their experiences and satisfaction with the facility's care and services.

- **Financial Considerations:** Understand the costs associated with residing in the ALF, including monthly fees, additional charges for specific services, and potential sources of financial assistance or insurance coverage.

By carefully considering these factors and conducting thorough research and visits, you can make an informed decision when choosing an ALF that best meets your or your loved one's needs and preferences.

CHAPTER 5: A LOCATION AND YOUR PERCEPTION

Assume for a minute you have decided on a location to review. Consider what is listed above. What are your thoughts when you approach this facility? Is the lawn cared for or if winter and you are in the north are the walks clear? What is the shape of the landscape? Remember this may be your home if it is your choice. A key factor in your choice is how far are you from your family's home. **<u>They will be your key helpers.</u>**

If you drive, is parking outside? What are your thoughts? If you don't drive, make sure you ask about transportation. **This is key.**

Reader's Notice: Most ALFs have their own definition of what is meant by furnished transportation. It may mean as a group to specific places like Walmart and not transportation to a specific place such as a medical facility. It may mean transportation will be handled by a contracted service. You must understand what you can expect from the ALF.

The family must pay close attention to the future resident's choice. See what he or she likes or does not like.

<u>KEEP THIS IN MIND:</u>
It is time to enter the ALF to see what your future home may look like. **Remember if this is your first visit to this facility it is going to be a sales pitch.** If this facility is of interest to you more than one visit is necessary. You cannot understand all aspects of what you must know on a first visit. **Do not be afraid to take notes or make a recording.**

As you entered this facility what were your thoughts? Were you impressed? Was it clean? Were you greeted by facility staff? Would you be proud of your location if visitors visited you in this location? Remember you are going to get a sales pitch. You are going to see the entire facility, but it will be in a limited time. Also remember you are here to learn so any question is valid. Naturally it is impossible to remember every question you may want to ask on this first visit. We do not know the actual layout for the facility in question so the author will simulate a tour addressing issues as we move on. Is this facility a single story or a multiple story? Does this influence your choice of a room based on individual needs? If this is a multiple story it will probably include independent living and memory care. Where in the building is ALF located? Is it close to dining and other areas used by all residents? What follows is a listing of locations that need minimal explanation for the first visit. If further information is needed it will follow this listing.

- **Dining:** will bring about the most complaints or issues for the facility. For the initial tour you may want to understand the number of meals served and if there are choices in the menu. Are meals served on a set schedule for each meal? We will get into more details in a later section of this book.

- **Kitchen:** In most ALFs the resident's kitchen will be equipped with a refrigerator, a microwave, counter space, and cupboards. It will be an open space to the living room.

- **Studios & Two-Bedroom Units:** may differ.

- **Hallways:** If they are long, they can be used for exercise such as walking or use of a walker. If you use a motorized vehicle can the hallway accommodate it with ease? The only issue here is how far do you have to go to get where you are going.

- **Elevator:** You want to keep in mind the location of the elevator if this is a multiple story building. Is there more than one elevator in the building? How far are they from places you will be using?

- **Family Rooms:** Most ALFs have multiple family rooms that residents may use for lunch with family or holiday get-togethers. Is there more than one family room? Will the size accommodate your family's needs? What furnishing does it have such as a kitchen, living room furniture, or television?

- **Exercise Room:** There is usually only one exercise room in a facility. What you need to review here is the type of equipment that the room has and if it is something you would use.

- **Meeting Rooms:** There are usually several meeting rooms in an ALF. These are used for resident or staff meetings. They also accommodate visitors who may be speaking or presenting at the ALF.

Here is where we must get serious even though it is the first visit. This is when the staff member takes you to the future resident's living quarters. You should have the choice of seeing a studio, one, or two bedrooms in most ALFs. You may see a three-bedroom room in some ALFs. Let us look at the resident's living quarters.

- **Resident Living Quarters**: When you first enter the resident's living quarters you will probably be surprised by the size as you may be moving from a single-family home. **This will be quite an adjustment for a new resident.** Take a careful look at your surroundings because if you choose this ALF, you will spend most of your time in this location. Think about what you plan to bring to the ALF. Do you think there is enough space to accommodate your belongings? If necessary, what items could you do without? You cannot figure all this out on the first visit but keep in mind what you see.

Your main thoughts should be about size. As you look at the kitchen, living room and bedroom spaces, ask yourself if your current furniture will fit and does the space allow for mobility devices if required now or in the future. The bathroom is usually directly off the bedroom. Here you need to take a quick look at the shower. Is it a walk-in? Does it have conveniently located handrails? Does it have room for a shower chair, if needed? Will you need assistance from the staff for use of the shower? Does the bathroom have sufficient storage space?

At this point we have learned some of the details about the ALF. What we need to do now is get into more detail and prepare for a follow-up tour of this or other ALFs. **Do not limit your search to a single ALF.** Yes, you may choose the first one you see as your choice but a second or third tour of others will only add to helping you make a choice. Let's look at more details.

- **Dining:**

  1. **Menu Variety and Flexibility:** Look for a diverse menu with options that accommodate various dietary preferences, restrictions, and cultural preferences. A flexible menu allows residents to choose meals that suit their tastes and nutritional needs.

  2. **Nutritional Quality:** Assess the nutritional quality of the meals provided, including the balance of macronutrients (carbohydrates, proteins, fats), variety of fruits and vegetables,

and portion sizes. Nutrient-rich meals are essential for supporting overall health and well-being, especially among seniors.

3. **Meal Planning and Special Diets:** Inquire about the process for meal planning and whether the facility can accommodate special diets such as vegetarian, vegan, low-sodium, diabetic-friendly, or texture-modified diets for residents with swallowing difficulties.

4. **Dining Experience:** Consider the ambiance and atmosphere of the dining areas, including seating arrangements, decor, cleanliness, and accessibility for residents with mobility aids. A pleasant dining experience enhances socialization, enjoyment, and overall satisfaction with meals.

5. **Mealtimes and Flexibility:** Evaluate the schedule for mealtimes and the flexibility to accommodate your preferences and routines. Some facilities offer extended meal hours or options for in-room dining to accommodate individual schedules.

6. **Dining Assistance and Support:** Assess the level of assistance and support provided to residents during mealtimes, including help with seating, menu selection, eating utensils, and feeding assistance for residents with physical or cognitive impairments.

7. **Resident Feedback and Satisfaction:** Seek feedback from current residents and their families regarding their dining experiences, meal quality, service responsiveness, and overall satisfaction with dining services. Resident input is valuable for identifying areas for improvement and ensuring continuous quality improvement.

8. **Culinary Staff and Training:** Inquire about the qualifications, training, and experience of culinary staff responsible for meal preparation and service. Well-trained chefs and dietary staff contribute to the quality and consistency of meals served.

9. **Special Events and Dining Programs:** Explore whether the facility offers special dining events, themed meals, holiday celebrations, or cooking demonstrations to enhance residents' dining experiences and social engagement.

10. **Health and Safety Measures:** Ensure that the facility adheres to food safety standards, sanitation protocols, and infection control

measures to minimize the risk of foodborne illnesses and ensure the health and safety of residents.

By considering these factors, residents and their families can make informed decisions about the dining services offered at an ALF, ensuring that mealtimes are enjoyable, nutritious, and supportive of residents' overall health and well-being.

Remember to evaluate this section with care. Food service will be your biggest issue for most residents in the ALF. Read the points above to form questions you may have. Then ASK THEM.

- ### Living Room and Family Room:

  I am going to address both the living room in your apartment and the family rooms which will be in the common areas. Of course, you will address your own living room in your apartment and the ALF will handle family rooms. You can use what is listed below to evaluate the family rooms.

  When evaluating the living room in an ALF, several factors should be considered to ensure it meets the needs and preferences of residents and promotes comfort, socialization, and relaxation. Here are key factors to consider: **Most ALFs will require you to provide your own furniture.**

  1. **Layout and Accessibility:** Assess the layout of the living room to ensure it is spacious, well-lit, and easily accessible for residents with mobility aids such as wheelchairs or walkers. Adequate space between furniture and clear pathways enhances mobility and safety.

  2. **Comfortable Seating:** Evaluate the comfort and functionality of the seating arrangements, including chairs, sofas, and recliners. Look for supportive seating with cushions, armrests, and ergonomic design to promote comfort during leisure activities and social gatherings.

  3. **Decor and Ambiance:** Consider the decor, furnishings, and ambiance of the living room, including colors, lighting, artwork, and decorations. A welcoming and homelike atmosphere enhances relaxation, enjoyment, and a sense of belonging among residents.

4. **Multi-Functional Spaces**: Look for living rooms that serve multiple purposes, such as socializing, recreational activities, reading, watching television, and hosting events or group activities. Flexible furniture arrangements and versatile design elements accommodate various resident preferences and interests.

5. **Accessibility to Amenities**: Assess the proximity of the living room to other amenities and common areas within the facility, such as dining areas, outdoor spaces, recreational facilities, and resident rooms. Convenient access encourages residents to participate in social activities and engage with their surroundings.

6. **Safety Features**: Ensure that the living room is equipped with safety features such as handrails, grab bars, slip-resistant flooring, and emergency call systems to promote the safety and well-being of residents, especially those with mobility or balance issues.

7. **Entertainment Options**: Explore the availability of entertainment options in the living room, including televisions, radios, board games, puzzles, books, and magazines. Access to diverse entertainment options fosters engagement, stimulation, and enjoyment among residents.

8. **Socialization Opportunities**: Consider the layout and design of the living room to facilitate social interaction and connection among residents. Group seating arrangements, conversation areas, and communal spaces encourage residents to interact, build friendships, and participate in community life.

9. **Cleanliness and Maintenance**: Observe the cleanliness, upkeep, and maintenance of the living room during visits. Clean and well-maintained surroundings promote comfort, hygiene, and a positive living environment for residents.

10. **Resident Feedback and Satisfaction**: Seek feedback from current residents and their families regarding their experiences in the living room, including comfort, accessibility, activities, and socialization opportunities. Resident input is valuable for identifying areas for improvement and ensuring that the living room meets the

diverse needs and preferences of residents.

By considering these factors, residents and their families can evaluate the living room in an ALF and determine whether it provides a welcoming, comfortable, and supportive environment that enhances residents' quality of life and well-being.

One last thing is, don't forget to look at the view from your living room of the resident quarters. It will be what you are looking at during your stay.

- **Bedroom:**
  Speaking of views don't forget to look at the view from your bedroom.

  When moving to an ALF, the bedroom becomes a central space where residents spend a significant portion of their time. Evaluating the bedroom is crucial to ensuring comfort, safety, and a sense of personal space. Here are key factors to consider when assessing the bedroom in an ALF:

  1. **Size and Layout:** Assess the size and layout of the bedroom to ensure it accommodates the resident's furniture, mobility aids, and personal belongings comfortably. Adequate space around the bed and furniture enhances accessibility and maneuverability within the room.

  2. **Accessibility Features:** Look for accessibility features such as wide doorways, grab bars, adjustable bed heights, and accessible closets and storage areas. These features promote independence and safety for residents with mobility challenges.

  3. **Natural Light and Ventilation:** Consider the availability of natural light and ventilation in the bedroom. Large windows or ample lighting sources brighten the space and contribute to a pleasant atmosphere, while proper ventilation ensures air quality and comfort.

  4. **Privacy:** Evaluate the level of privacy provided in the bedroom, including soundproofing, window treatments, and door locks. Residents should feel secure and have the option to personalize their space to suit their privacy preferences.

5. **Furnishings and Amenities**: Assess the quality and condition of furnishings provided in the bedroom, including the bed, mattress, nightstands, dresser, and seating. Comfortable and functional furnishings contribute to a restful and inviting environment. **Remember most ALFs require the resident to furnish the furniture for this room.**

6. **Storage Space**: Evaluate the availability of storage space in the bedroom, including closets, drawers, and shelves. Sufficient storage allows residents to organize their belongings and maintain a clutter-free living environment.

7. **Safety Features:** Ensure that the bedroom is equipped with safety features such as smoke detectors, emergency call systems, and well-lit pathways. These features promote the safety and well-being of residents, especially during nighttime or in case of emergencies.

8. **Personalization Options:** Inquire about the flexibility to personalize the bedroom with the resident's own furnishings, decorations, and mementos. Personal touches create a sense of familiarity, identity, and homeliness in the new living environment.

9. **Temperature Control**: Verify the availability of temperature control options in the bedroom, such as thermostats or climate control systems. Residents should have the ability to adjust the temperature to their comfort preferences year-round.

10. **Resident Feedback and Satisfaction: Seek feedback from current residents and their families regarding their experiences in the bedroom, including comfort, cleanliness, and functionality. Resident input is valuable for identifying any issues or improvements needed to enhance the bedroom environment.**

Remember you most likely will be furnishing your own furniture.
By considering these factors, residents and their families can ensure that the bedroom in an ALF provides a comfortable, safe, and personalized living space that supports their well-being and quality of life.

- **Bathroom:**

When moving to an ALF, evaluating the bathroom and shower facilities is essential for ensuring safety, accessibility, and comfort. Here are key factors to consider when assessing the bathroom and shower amenities:

1. **Accessibility:** Features: Look for accessibility features in the bathroom, such as grab bars, non-slip flooring, and wheelchair-friendly layouts. These features promote safety and independence for residents with mobility challenges.

2. **Shower Accessibility:** Assess the accessibility of the shower area, including step-in or roll-in shower options, adjustable showerheads, and seating arrangements. Residents should be able to enter and use the shower safely and comfortably, with accommodations available for those with mobility impairments.

3. **Bathroom Layout:** Evaluate the layout of the bathroom to ensure there is sufficient space for maneuvering mobility aids and performing personal care tasks. Clear pathways and ample clearance around fixtures enhance accessibility and safety.

4. **Safety Features:** Ensure that the bathroom is equipped with safety features such as grab bars near the toilet and shower, non-slip mats or surfaces, and temperature-controlled water faucets. These features reduce the risk of slips, falls, and accidents.

5. **Personal Care Assistance:** Inquire about the availability of personal care assistance for residents who require help with bathing, toileting, and grooming. Trained staff members should be available to aid and support while respecting resident's dignity and privacy.

6. **Hygiene and Cleanliness:** Observe the cleanliness and hygiene standards of the bathroom and shower facilities during visits. Clean and well-maintained spaces promote comfort, health, and overall well-being for 's.

7. **Privacy:** Assess the level of privacy provided in the bathroom and shower areas, including locking doors, soundproofing, and visual barriers. Residents should feel comfortable and secure while using these facilities.

8. **Emergency Call Systems**: Verify the presence of emergency call systems or pull cords in the bathroom and shower areas. These systems enable residents to summon assistance quickly in case of emergencies or accidents.

9. **Personalization Options:** Inquire about the flexibility to personalize the bathroom and shower with the resident's own toiletries, towels, and accessories. Personal touches create a sense of familiarity and comfort in the new living environment.

10. **Resident Feedback and Satisfaction**: Seek feedback from current residents and their families regarding their experiences with the bathroom and shower facilities, including accessibility, cleanliness, and satisfaction. Resident input is valuable for identifying any areas for improvement or adjustments needed to enhance the bathroom experience.

By considering these factors, residents and their families can ensure that the bathroom and shower facilities in an ALF meet their needs and preferences, promoting safety, comfort, and dignity in daily personal care routines.

CHAPTER 6: BROCHURES AND MARKETING MATERIALS

We have had a more detailed look into what you should observe in various areas of the ALF. These details are for a visit that would occur after the first visit. Now let us look at some housekeeping tasks that will supplement your knowledge of the ALF and allow you to gain a greater understanding of the ALF you are evaluating. We will flip back and forth between the first visit and visits that follow.

On your first visit to an ALF, it's important to gather relevant information and documents to help you make an informed decision about the facility. Here are some key documents you should consider asking for during your visit:

- **<u>Brochures and Marketing Materials:</u>** Request brochures, pamphlets, or marketing materials provided by the facility. These documents typically provide an overview of the services, amenities, and features offered by the ALF, giving you a general idea of what to expect.

- **<u>Admission Agreement/Residency Contract:</u>** Ask for a copy of the admission agreement or residency contract. This document outlines the terms and conditions of residency, including fees, services provided, rules and regulations, and policies related to admission, discharge, and resident rights.

- **<u>Resident Handbook:</u>** Inquire about a resident handbook or guidebook that provides detailed information about the facility's policies, procedures, and expectations for residents. This document may cover topics such as visiting hours, meal schedules, activities, emergency procedures, and resident rights.

- **<u>Licensing and Certification:</u>** Request information about the facility's licensing, accreditation, and certification status from relevant regulatory agencies. This may include state licensing documents, inspection reports, and accreditation certificates, which can help you assess the facility's compliance with quality and safety standards.

- **Financial Disclosure:** Ask for details about the facility's fee structure, payment options, and any additional charges or fees associated with residency. This may include information about base monthly fees, levels of care fees, medication management fees, and any other charges for specific services or amenities.

- **Resident Rights and Grievance Procedures**: Inquire about documents outlining residents' rights, responsibilities, and grievance procedures. These documents should provide information about how a resident can voice concerns, file complaints, or seek resolution for issues related to their care, treatment, or living conditions.

- **Staffing and Training Credentials:** Request information about the qualifications, training, and credentials of staff members responsible for resident care and support. This may include details about licensed nurses, certified nursing assistants, caregivers, activity coordinators, and other personnel involved in resident services.

- **Health and Safety Policies**: Ask for copies of the facility's health and safety policies, including protocols for medication management, emergency preparedness, infection control, and resident care planning. These documents can help you understand how the facility maintains a safe and healthy environment for residents. **A resident may manage their own medication, have medication management by a family member or have ALF provide the service.**

- **Sample Menus and Dining Policies:** Inquire about sample menus, dining policies, and meal service options offered by the facility. This may include information about mealtimes, dietary accommodations, special diets, and options for resident input or customization of menus.

- **Resident Activities Calendar:** Request a copy of the facility's activities calendar or schedule of events. This document outlines the recreational, social, and educational activities available to residents, helping you assess the variety and frequency of engagement opportunities.

Ask for several weeks of past menu and activity schedules. You are looking for a trend. By requesting these documents during your first visit to an ALF, you can gather valuable information to help you evaluate the facility's services, policies, and environment, and make an informed decision about whether it meets your or your loved one's needs and preferences.

CHAPTER 7: IMPORTANT DOCUMENTS

After your first visit you may request other documents that relate to the operations of the ALF. I would assume not every document requested will be delivered. You may want to request additional documents to further assess the facility and make an informed decision. Here are some documents you should consider requesting. This may appear the author is repeating some requests. What the author is trying to point out these documents are important for any future resident.

- **<u>Resident Agreement/Contract:</u>** Obtain a copy of the resident agreement or contract if you haven't already received it. Review this document carefully to understand the terms and conditions of residency, including fees, services provided, and resident rights.

- **<u>Admission Criteria</u>:** Request information about the facility's admission criteria and eligibility requirements. Understanding the criteria for admission can help you determine if the facility is suitable for your or your loved one's needs.

- **<u>Floor Plans and Room Layouts:</u>** Ask for floor plans or room layouts to get a better sense of the available living spaces and amenities. Reviewing these documents can help you visualize the layout of the facility and determine which rooms may be most suitable. If you get a resident's book on your first visit it is quite possible you will have floor plan drawing of the various apartments.

- **<u>Resident Care Plans:</u>** Inquire about the facility's process for developing and implementing resident care plans. Request sample care plans or information about how individualized care is provided to residents based on their needs and preferences.

- **<u>Staffing Ratios and Qualifications:</u>** Request details about the facility's staffing ratios and the qualifications of staff members. Understand the ratio of caregivers to residents and inquire about staff training, certifications, and experience in providing care to seniors.

- **Health Services and Support:** Obtain information about the health services and support available at the facility. Request details about medication management, assistance with ADLs, healthcare coordination, and access to medical professionals.

- **Resident Handbook or Policies:** Ask for a copy of the facility's resident handbook or policies and procedures manual. Reviewing these documents can provide valuable information about resident rights, responsibilities, and expectations for living in the facility.

- **Financial Disclosure and Fee Structure:** Request additional details about the facility's fee structure, payment policies, and any additional charges or fees. Understand how fees are calculated, what is included in the base rate, and how payment arrangements are managed.

- **Inspection Reports and Compliance History:** Inquire about the facility's compliance history and any recent inspection reports from regulatory agencies. Reviewing these documents can help you assess the facility's track record for meeting quality and safety standards.

- **References or Testimonials:** Ask for references or testimonials from current or former residents and their families. Hearing about others' experiences with the facility can provide valuable insights into the quality of care and services provided.

By requesting these documents after your first visit to an ALF, you can gather additional information to help you evaluate the facility and make an informed decision about whether it meets your or your loved one's needs and preferences. **The more you know about the facility the better off you are.** Naturally you do not need all this information if you have no interest in the ALF you are touring.

CHAPTER 8: DAILY ROUTINES

Daily routines and activities in an ALF are designed to promote engagement, socialization, wellness, and a sense of purpose among residents. While specific activities may vary depending on the facility's resources, resident preferences, and programming. Here are common elements of daily routines and activities in ALFs:

- **MORNING ROUTINE:**

    1. **Breakfast:** Residents typically gather in dining areas for breakfast, which may be served buffet-style or as a seated meal.

    2. **Personal Care**: Staff assist residents with morning personal care routines such as bathing, grooming, dressing, and medication management.

    3. **Exercise:** Some facilities offer morning exercise classes or gentle fitness activities to promote physical health and mobility

- **DAYTIME ACTIVITIES:**

    1. **Socialization:** Throughout the day, residents have opportunities for socialization with peers, staff, and visiting family members. This may include conversations, games, or shared meals.

    2. **Recreational Activities:** ALFs offer a variety of recreational activities to cater to residents' interests and abilities. These may include arts and crafts, gardening, music therapy, pet therapy, baking, and puzzles.

    3. **Educational Programs:** Many facilities host educational programs, lectures, or discussion groups on topics of interest to residents, such as history, current events, or wellness.

4. **Outings and Excursions:** Some ALFs organize outings to local attractions, shopping centers, restaurants, parks, or cultural events to provide residents with opportunities for community engagement and leisure.

- **AFTERNOON ROUTINE:**

1. **Lunch:** Residents gather for lunch, which may include a hot meal, salad bar, or sandwich options.

2. **Rest and Relaxation:** Afternoon downtime allows residents to rest, read, or engage in quiet activities in their rooms or common areas.

- **EVENING ACTIVITIES:**

1. **Dinner:** Dinner is served in dining areas, providing residents with an opportunity to socialize and enjoy an evening meal together.

2. **Entertainment:** Evenings may feature entertainment such as live music performances, movie nights, trivia contests, or themed parties.

3. **Relaxation:** Residents can unwind in common areas, outdoor spaces, or their own rooms before bedtime.

- **SPECIAL EVENTS AND CELEBRATIONS:**

1. ALFs often host special events and celebrations to mark holidays, birthdays, or milestones. These may include parties, concerts, dances, or festive meals.

- **PERSONALIZED CARE AND SERVICES:**

1. In addition to structured activities, ALFs provide personalized care and services tailored to each resident's individual needs and preferences. This may include assistance with daily living activities, healthcare coordination, medication management, and emotional support.

2. The daily routines and activities in an ALF should enhance the resident's quality of life, foster a sense of community, and promote physical, emotional, and cognitive well-being. By

offering a diverse range of engaging and meaningful activities, ALFs strive to create vibrant living environments where residents can thrive and enjoy a fulfilling lifestyle.

- ## HEALTH AND WELLNESS:

1. Remember an ALF is not a nursing home. Resources will vary by ALF. If you have questions, ask. **Readers Notice: Most people have habits they want to continue. If you have habits such as a daily shower at a special period of the day, can the ALF meet that requirement? ASK THEM!**

- ## HEALTHCARE SERVICES:

1. **ALFs Healthcare Services:** are typically designed to support a residents' health and well-being while promoting independence and quality of life. While the specific healthcare services offered can vary depending on the facility's resources, licensing, and resident needs, here are some common healthcare services provided in most ALFs:

2. **Medication Management:** ALFs often help with medication management, including medication reminders, assistance with medication administration, and monitoring for potential side effects or interactions. Trained staff members help ensure that residents take their medications as prescribed by their healthcare providers.

3. **Personal Care Assistance:** Many ALFs provide personal care assistance to help residents with ADLs such as bathing, dressing, grooming, toileting, and mobility. Caregivers offer support and supervision based on individual needs and preferences, promoting resident's comfort, dignity, and independence.

4. **Health Monitoring:** ALFs may offer health monitoring services to track a resident's health status, vital signs, and changes in condition. This may include regular health assessments, monitoring chronic conditions, and coordinating with healthcare providers to address any health concerns or changes.

5. **Healthcare Coordination:** ALFs often facilitate healthcare coordination by coordinating appointments, arranging transportation to medical appointments, and communicating with resident's healthcare providers. This ensures continuity of care

and promotes collaboration between the ALF staff and external healthcare professionals.

6. **Emergency Response:** ALFs are equipped to respond to medical emergencies and provide emergency care as needed. This may include access to emergency call systems, trained staff members available 24/7, and protocols for responding to medical emergencies such as falls, injuries, or sudden illnesses.

7. **Wellness Programs:** Many ALFs offer wellness programs and health promotion initiatives to support residents' overall health and well-being. This may include exercise classes, fitness programs, nutrition education, preventive health screenings, and opportunities for socialization and engagement.

8. **Therapy Services:** Some ALFs offer therapy services such as physical therapy, occupational therapy, or speech therapy on-site or through partnerships with external providers. These services aim to improve a resident's functional abilities, mobility, and independence in daily activities.

9. **Memory Care:** For residents with dementia or alzheimer's disease, specialized memory care services may be available within ALFs memory care programs provide tailored support, structured activities, and a safe environment designed to meet the unique needs of individuals with memory impairments.

10. **Palliative Care and End-of-Life Support:** ALFs may offer palliative care services to manage pain and symptoms, enhance comfort, and improve quality of life for residents with serious illnesses or advanced age. End-of-life support may include hospice services, emotional support for residents and families, and assistance with advance care planning.

11. **Health Education and Support:** ALFs often provide health education and support services to empower residents and their families to make informed decisions about their health and wellness. This may include educational workshops, support groups, access to health-related resources, and assistance with navigating healthcare systems.

By offering a range of healthcare services tailored to a resident's needs, ALFs strive to promote holistic wellness, independence, and quality of life for residents while ensuring access to appropriate care and support as needed.

CHAPTER 9: CARING IN AN ASSISTED LIVING FACILITY

CAREGIVING IN AN ALF:

Remember the thing you read under this section may relate to one ALF but not another. Use this section to see what may be of interest to you. **Then if you need information from the ALF you are evaluating, ASK.** Caregiving in an ALF plays a crucial role in supporting a resident's health, well-being, and independence.

Caregivers in ALFs provide a range of services tailored to meet a resident's individual needs and preferences. Here's an overview of caregiving in an ALF: Again, some of this has been discussed by the author, but is stated to offer the reader a list of what is usually provided by the ALF.

- **Personal Care Assistance:** Caregivers assist residents with ADLs such as bathing, dressing, grooming, toileting, and mobility. They provide hands-on support and encouragement while respecting the resident's privacy, dignity, and autonomy.

- **Medication Management:** Caregivers help residents manage their medications safely and effectively. This may include medication reminders, assistance with medication administration, and monitoring for potential side effects or interactions. Caregivers ensure that residents take their medications as prescribed by their healthcare providers.

- **Health Monitoring:** Caregivers monitor residents' health status, vital signs, and changes in condition. They observe for signs of discomfort, illness, or decline and communicate any concerns to appropriate staff members or healthcare providers. Regular health assessments and documentation help track residents' health status over time.

- **<u>Emotional Support</u>:** Caregivers provide emotional support and companionship to residents, fostering a sense of connection, belonging, and well-being. They listen attentively to a resident's concerns, offer empathy and reassurance, and engage in meaningful conversations to promote socialization and engagement.

- **<u>Assistance with Meals</u>:** Caregivers assist residents with meal preparation, dining assistance, and nutrition support. They ensure that residents have access to nutritious and appetizing meals that meet their dietary preferences, restrictions, and cultural needs. Caregivers may also provide feeding assistance for residents who require help with eating or swallowing.

- **<u>Mobility Support</u>:** Caregivers help residents maintain mobility and independence by aiding with walking, transferring, and using mobility aids such as walkers, wheelchairs, or canes. They offer encouragement, supervision, and physical assistance as needed to promote safety and confidence.

- **<u>Healthcare Coordination</u>:** Caregivers coordinate residents' healthcare needs by scheduling appointments, arranging transportation to medical visits, and communicating with healthcare providers. They advocate for residents' health and well-being, ensuring that they receive appropriate medical care and follow-up as needed.

- **<u>Emergency Response</u>:** Caregivers are trained to respond to medical emergencies and provide first aid or emergency care as needed. They are knowledgeable about emergency protocols, including how to access emergency services, administer CPR, and use emergency call systems within the facility.

- **<u>Resident Advocacy</u>:** Caregivers serve as advocates for residents, ensuring that their rights, preferences, and wishes are respected and upheld. They collaborate with residents, families, and interdisciplinary teams to develop care plans that promote individualized, person-centered care.

- **<u>Documentation and Reporting</u>:** Caregivers maintain accurate and detailed documentation of resident care activities, observations, and interactions. They document changes in a resident's health status, behaviors, and preferences, and report any concerns to appropriate staff members for follow-up and intervention.

Overall, caregiving in an ALF encompasses a holistic approach to supporting a resident's' physical, emotional, and social well-being. Caregivers play a vital role in creating a supportive and nurturing environment where residents can thrive, maintain independence, and enjoy a fulfilling quality of life.

Readers Notice. The information under "<u>CAREGIVING IN AN AFL</u>", is seen by the author as the ideal situation. However, there are some facilities that may not meet the ideal situations. Take the time to review with the proper staff of the facility you are evaluating their procedures for providing care and handling emergency situations. This is a must requirement.

CHAPTER 10: MAINTAINING INDEPENDENCE

<u>MAINTAINING INDEPENDENCE:</u>

It is important for most people to have their own self-time. Over my time in an, I have met many individuals who paint, draw, use a computer or write books. Listed below are suggestions for you to consider. Maintaining independence in an ALF is important for residents' well-being and quality of life. While residents may require assistance with certain tasks or activities, there are several ways to preserve independence within an ALF setting:

- **<u>Communicate Your Preferences:</u>** Clearly communicate your preferences, needs, and expectations with staff members and caregivers. Advocate for yourself and express your desire to remain as independent as possible while receiving support as needed.

- **<u>Participate in Decision-Making:</u>** Take an active role in decisions about your care, daily routines, activities, and lifestyle choices. Participate in care planning meetings, discuss your goals and preferences with staff members, and collaborate on creating personalized care plans that respect your autonomy.

- **<u>Maintain Personal Routines:</u>** Maintain your personal routines and habits as much as possible within the ALF environment. Stick to familiar routines for activities such as waking up, bathing, dressing, meals, and leisure pursuits, which can promote a sense of familiarity and continuity.

- **<u>Stay Engaged in Activities:</u>** Engage in activities and social opportunities offered by the ALF that align with your interests, hobbies, and preferences. Participating in group activities, outings, classes, and events fosters social connections, stimulation, and a sense of purpose.

- **<u>Advocate for Supportive Services:</u>** Advocate for supportive services and accommodations that enhance your independence and well-being. This may include requesting assistive devices, adaptive equipment, or modifications to your living space that improve accessibility and functionality.

- **Learn Self-Care Strategies:** Learn and practice self-care strategies that promote independence and self-reliance. This may include techniques for managing ADLs, practicing safe mobility skills, and utilizing assistive devices or adaptive techniques to overcome challenges.

- **Seek Assistance Wisely:** Be proactive in seeking assistance from staff members or caregivers when needed, but also recognize your own capabilities and limitations. Request assistance with tasks that are difficult or unsafe to perform independently, while maintaining autonomy in areas where you can manage on your own.

- **Stay Informed:** Stay informed about your rights, responsibilities, and options within the ALF setting. Familiarize yourself with facility policies, procedures, and resources available to residents. Seek information and support from staff members, resident councils, or advocacy organizations as needed.

- **Foster Independence in Daily Tasks:** Look for opportunities to engage in tasks and activities that promote independence and self-sufficiency. Practice activities such as **meal preparation, laundry, housekeeping, and managing personal finances** (many of these activities can be provided by the ALF. to maintain skills and autonomy.

- **Build a Support Network:** Build a support network of family members, friends, and fellow residents who respect your independence and offer encouragement, companionship, and assistance when needed. Cultivate relationships that provide emotional support, social connection, and a sense of belonging within the ALF community.

By actively advocating for yourself, participating in decision-making, staying engaged in activities, and utilizing support services wisely, you can maintain a sense of independence and control over your daily life while living in an ALF.

CHAPTER 11: FINANCIAL AND LEGAL CONSIDERATIONS

When considering moving into an ALF, there are several important legal and financial considerations to consider. These factors can have significant implications for your long-term care, financial security, and overall well-being. Here are some key considerations:

- **Admission Agreement/Residency Contract:** Review the admission agreement or residency contract carefully before signing. Pay close attention to the terms and conditions of residency, including fees, services provided, rules and regulations, and policies related to admission, discharge, and resident rights.

- **Cost of Care:** Understand the cost of care associated with living in the ALF, including base monthly fees, levels of care fees, medication management fees, and any additional charges for specific services or amenities. Clarify what is included in the base rate and what services may incur extra costs.

- **Payment Options:** Explore payment options for covering the cost of care, including private pay, long-term care insurance, Medicaid, Veterans benefits, and other sources of financial assistance. Determine which payment options are available to you and how they align with your financial resources and preferences.

- **Financial Planning:** Evaluate your financial situation and consider how moving into an ALF will impact your long-term financial security. Develop a financial plan that addresses potential costs of care, housing expenses, healthcare expenses, and other financial obligations.

- **Medicaid Eligibility:** If you anticipate needing Medicaid to help cover the cost of care in the future, understand the eligibility requirements and Medicaid rules specific to ALF coverage in your state. Seek guidance from a financial advisor or elder law attorney to navigate Medicaid planning and eligibility.

Readers Notice: Most ALFs require a two-year private pay in their facility before they will accept payment by a support source such as Medicare. Are you able to meet this requirement? Think about it as you evaluate your financial status.

- **<u>Advance Directives</u>:** Ensure that your advance directives, including a healthcare proxy, living will, and durable power of attorney for healthcare, are up-to-date and reflect your wishes regarding medical treatment, end-of-life care, and decision-making in the event of incapacity.

- **<u>Estate Planning</u>:** Review your estate planning documents, including wills, trusts, and beneficiary designations, to ensure they align with your current wishes and circumstances. Consider how moving into an ALF may impact your estate planning goals and arrangements for inheritance and asset distribution.

- **<u>Legal Protections</u>:** Familiarize yourself with legal protections for residents of ALFs, including residents' rights, grievance procedures, and regulatory oversight. Understand how state and local laws govern ALFs and ensure that your rights are respected and upheld.

- **<u>Insurance Coverage</u>:** Review your existing insurance coverage, including health insurance, long-term care insurance, Medicare, and supplemental insurance policies. Understand what services and expenses are covered by your insurance plans and whether any adjustments or additional coverage is needed.

- **<u>Consultation with Professionals</u>:** Seek guidance from legal, financial, and healthcare professionals who specialize in elder law, estate planning, long-term care planning, and insurance matters. These professionals can provide personalized advice and assistance tailored to your specific needs and circumstances.

There is no free lunch in an ALF. Long-Term Insurance does expire. Be ready for those days. By addressing these legal and financial considerations proactively, you can make informed decisions about moving into an ALF, protect your interests, and ensure that you have the necessary support and resources to navigate the transition and

maintain your well-being in the long term. Read with care.

CHAPTER12: COMMUNITY AND SOCIAL CONNECTIONS

ALF residents are often asked to volunteer in church, schools, or nonprofit community events if they are able and interested. Such activities can also contribute to your own independence. Think about this. Engaging in volunteer work and community events can offer numerous benefits for residents, including socialization, purposeful activity, and a sense of fulfillment. Here's how residents can participate:

- **Volunteer Services:** Many ALFs facilitate opportunities for residents to engage in volunteer work within the facility or in the broader community. Residents may volunteer their time and talents to assist with activities such as crafting, gardening, reading to children, or visiting with other residents who may benefit from companionship and support.

- **Community Events:** ALFs often organize or sponsor community events, outings, and activities that residents can participate in. These events may include attending cultural performances, art exhibits, concerts, lectures, or local festivals. Residents may also have the opportunity to participate in community service projects or charitable initiatives.

- **Resident-Led Activities:** Residents can take the initiative to organize and lead activities, events, or groups within the ALF community. This may include forming clubs, discussion groups, hobby circles, or special interest groups based on shared interests or experiences. Resident-led activities can foster a sense of camaraderie and empowerment among residents.

- **Intergenerational Programs:** ALFs may collaborate with schools, youth organizations, or other community groups to facilitate intergenerational programs and activities. Residents may participate in mentoring, tutoring, or sharing their skills and life experiences with younger generations. Intergenerational interactions can enrich residents' lives and promote meaningful connections across age groups.

- **<u>Transportation Assistance</u>:** ALFs often provide transportation services or arrange for transportation to facilitate residents' participation in volunteer services and community events. This may include shuttle services, group outings, or assistance with arranging transportation for individual residents who wish to participate in specific activities. Ask about and understand the transportation program. It will vary from one ALF to another. Know what to expect.

- **<u>Flexible Scheduling</u>:** ALFs strive to accommodate residents' preferences and schedules when planning activities and events. Flexible scheduling allows residents to participate in volunteer services and community events based on their availability, interests, and energy levels.

- **<u>Supportive Environment</u>:** ALF staff members and fellow residents provide encouragement, assistance, and support to residents who wish to participate in volunteer services and community events. Staff members may help coordinate logistics, provide transportation, or assist with any accommodations needed to ensure residents can fully engage in activities.

By participating in volunteer services and community events, residents in ALFs can stay connected to their communities, maintain a sense of purpose and belonging, and contribute meaningfully to the well-being of others. These opportunities for engagement promote socialization, stimulation, and a sense of fulfillment, enhancing residents' overall quality of life.

CHAPTER 13: FAMILY EXPECTATIONS

What would you expect of your family? They will be with you in this situation. Family connections and family support play a significant role in the experience of individuals living in ALFs. Here's how family connections and support can impact residents in ALFs:

- **Emotional Support**: Family members provide emotional support to residents, offering companionship, encouragement, and reassurance. Regular visits, phone calls, and meaningful interactions with family members help residents feel connected, loved, and valued.

- **Advocacy and Communication:** Family members serve as advocates for residents, ensuring that their needs, preferences, and concerns are communicated effectively to ALF staff members and addressed promptly. Family members may attend care planning meetings, discuss treatment options with healthcare providers, and collaborate on decision-making regarding the resident's care and well-being.

- **Assistance with Activities**: Family members may assist residents with various activities, such as attending appointments, running errands, managing finances, or arranging transportation for outings or social events. This support enhances residents' independence, mobility, and access to community resources.

- **Involvement in Caregiving:** Family members may be actively involved in providing care and assistance to residents, supplementing the services provided by the ALF staff members. This may include helping with personal care tasks, medication management, or monitoring the resident's health and well-being.

- **Information Sharing:** Family members provide valuable information to ALF staff members about the resident's preferences, routines, medical history, and care needs. Sharing insights and updates with staff members helps ensure that the resident receives personalized, person-centered care that aligns with their individual preferences and wishes.

- **<u>Decision-Making Support:</u>** Family members participate in important decisions related to the resident's care, treatment, and living arrangements. They collaborate with ALF staff members and healthcare providers to make informed decisions about healthcare interventions, end-of-life care, and other significant matters affecting the resident's well-being.

- **<u>Social Connection:</u>** Family members contribute to residents' social connectedness by facilitating visits with relatives, organizing family gatherings or celebrations, and involving residents in family events and traditions. These interactions promote socialization, engagement, and a sense of belonging within the family unit.

- **<u>Respite Care and Support:</u>** Family members may rely on ALFs to provide respite care and support when they need temporary relief from caregiving responsibilities. ALFs offer short-term stays or respite care services, allowing family caregivers to take breaks, attend to their own needs, or address other obligations while ensuring that their loved one receives quality care and support in their absence.

Overall, family connections and support play a vital role in enhancing the quality of life, well-being, and satisfaction of residents living in assisted living facilities. By fostering strong family relationships, ALFs create a supportive and nurturing environment that promotes a resident's physical, emotional, and social well-being.

CHAPTER 14: END OF LIFE PLANNING

End of life planning. It will happen. Do not avoid this important topic.

When discussing end-of-life planning with your family, it's important to cover a range of topics to ensure that your wishes, preferences, and practical arrangements are clearly communicated and understood. Here are some key topics to include in these discussions:

- **Advance Directives:** Discuss your wishes regarding medical treatment and end-of-life care, including the use of life-sustaining measures, resuscitation preferences, and preferences for palliative care or hospice care. Ensure that your advance directives, including a living will and healthcare proxy, accurately reflect your wishes and are accessible to family members and healthcare providers.

- **Funeral and Burial Preferences:** Share your preferences for funeral arrangements, burial or cremation, and any specific requests regarding memorial services or rituals. Discuss whether you have made arrangements in advance, such as pre-paid funeral plans or burial plots, and ensure that your family members are aware of these arrangements.

- **Financial and Legal Matters:** Review important financial and legal documents with your family, including wills, trusts, powers of attorney, and beneficiary designations. Discuss your wishes for the distribution of assets, management of finances, and any specific instructions or considerations regarding estate planning and probate.

- **End-of-Life Care Planning:** Discuss your preferences for end-of-life care, including where you would like to receive care (e.g., at home, in a hospice facility, in an ALF, who you would like to be involved in your care, and any specific goals or priorities for your comfort and quality of life during this time.

- **<u>Family Roles and Responsibilities</u>:** Clarify roles and responsibilities among family members regarding decision-making, caregiving, and support during your end-of-life journey. Discuss how family members can work together as a team to ensure that your wishes are respected and implemented effectively.

- **<u>Emotional and Spiritual Support:</u>** Address emotional and spiritual needs with your family, including opportunities for meaningful connections, expressions of love and gratitude, and support for coping with grief and loss. Discuss how family members can provide emotional support to one another and honor your legacy and memory.

- **<u>Healthcare Proxy and Durable Power of Attorney:</u>** Designate a healthcare proxy and durable power of attorney to make medical and financial decisions on your behalf if you become incapacitated. Discuss your choice of proxy with your family and ensure that they understand their roles and responsibilities in these capacities.

- **<u>Communication and Documentation:</u>** Establish clear channels of communication with your family members and ensure that important documents, instructions, and contact information are readily accessible and organized. Discuss how family members can access relevant information and communicate with healthcare providers, legal advisors, and other relevant parties.

- **<u>Cultural and Religious Considerations</u>:** Consider cultural and religious beliefs and traditions that may influence your end-of-life preferences and rituals. Discuss how your cultural or religious values can be honored and respected during the end-of-life planning process and memorial arrangements.

- **<u>Review and Update:</u>** Regularly review and update your end-of-life plans and preferences as circumstances change and communicate any updates or revisions with your family members. Encourage open and ongoing communication to ensure that everyone remains informed and prepared for the future.

By addressing these topics with your family, you can ensure that your end-of-life wishes are understood, respected, and implemented in accordance with your values and preferences. Open and honest communication lays the foundation for a supportive and meaningful end-of-life experience for both you and your loved ones.

CHAPTER15: FUTURE TRENDS IN ASSISTED LIVING

Several trends are shaping the future of ALFs as they continue to evolve to meet the changing needs and preferences of older adults. Here are some key trends in the ALF industry:

- **Personalized and Person-Centered Care:** There is a growing emphasis on providing personalized care and services tailored to each resident's individual needs, preferences, and goals. ALFs are adopting person-centered care approaches that prioritize resident choice, autonomy, and dignity, fostering a more empowering and fulfilling living experience.

- **Enhanced Wellness and Holistic Care:** ALFs are expanding their focus beyond traditional medical care to promote holistic wellness and well-being among residents. This includes incorporating wellness programs, preventive health initiatives, nutrition and fitness programs, and holistic therapies such as massage, acupuncture, and mindfulness practices to support a resident's physical, emotional, and spiritual health.

- **Technology Integration:** Technology is increasingly being integrated into ALFs to enhance resident safety, communication, and quality of life. This includes the use of electronic health records (EHRs), telemedicine services, remote monitoring systems, wearable devices, smart home technologies, and communication platforms to improve care coordination, enable virtual social connections, and provide timely assistance to residents.

- **Aging in Place and Continuum of Care:** ALFs are offering expanded services and amenities to support aging in place and accommodate a resident's changing care needs over time. Many facilities are incorporating memory care units, skilled nursing care, rehabilitation services, and hospice care options on-site or through partnerships with external providers, allowing residents to remain in familiar surroundings as their care needs evolve.

- **Innovative Design and Amenities:** ALFs are embracing innovative design concepts and amenities to create supportive, inviting, and age-friendly environments for residents. This includes features such as universal design principles, barrier-free environments, outdoor spaces, therapeutic gardens, communal living areas, and technology-enabled amenities that promote socialization, engagement, and independence.

- **Diverse Housing Options':** There is a wider range of housing options to accommodate diverse preferences and lifestyles among older adults. This includes studio apartments, one-bedroom or two-bedroom units, shared living arrangements, independent living cottages, and age-in-place models that provide flexible housing solutions based on individual needs and preferences.

- **Cultural Competency and Inclusivity:** ALFs are recognizing the importance of cultural competency and inclusivity in serving a diverse resident population. They are implementing culturally sensitive care practices, language assistance services, diverse programming, and inclusive policies to ensure that residents from diverse backgrounds feel respected, valued, and supported in the ALF community.

- **Sustainability and Environmental Stewardship:** ALFs are prioritizing sustainability and environmental stewardship in their operations and practices. This includes adopting green building standards, energy-efficient technologies, recycling and waste reduction initiatives, and sustainable landscaping practices to minimize environmental impact and create healthier living environments for residents.

- **Collaboration and Partnerships:** ALFs are forming collaborative partnerships with healthcare providers, community organizations, academia, and other stakeholders to enhance resident care, expand service offerings, and address emerging challenges in aging services. These partnerships foster interdisciplinary collaboration, knowledge sharing, and innovation in ALF care delivery and programming.

- **Regulatory and Policy Changes:** ALFs are adapting to evolving regulatory and policy changes at the state and federal levels that impact licensing, quality standards, reimbursement models, and resident rights. Facilities are staying informed about regulatory requirements, industry best practices, and emerging trends to ensure compliance and maintain high standards of care and service delivery.

Overall, the future of ALFs is characterized by a commitment to person centered care, innovation, inclusivity, and sustainability, as facilities strive to create supportive empowering, and vibrant living environments that enhance the well-being and quality of life for older adults.

I hope you enjoyed this book and now have a better understanding of your search. Thank you.

9 798325 778612